BIRDS + BEES + *YOUR* KIDS

A Guide to Sharing Your Beliefs About Sexuality, Love and Relationships

Everything YOU need to know before they start middle school!

Amy Lang, MA

Birds + Bees + Kids® LLC

BirdsAndBeesAndKids.com

1st Edition Copyright 2009 by Amy Lang MA

2nd Edition Copyright 2016 by Amy Lang, MA

Birds + Bees + Kids® and the Bird + Bees logo are registered trademarks.

ISBN-13: 978-1539013266

ISBN-10: 153901326X

TABLE OF CONTENTS

Introduction – *My Story*...iii

Section One – *Your story, beliefs, hopes and dreams*

Chapter 1
Sexuality + Values – What Do You Believe?...........................3

Chapter 2
Your Story – How You Learned about The Birds + The Bees.... 9

Chapter 3
Love + Healthy Relationships.......................................13

Chapter 4
What Does "Ready for Sex" Mean to You?........................... 17

Chapter 5
Why Wait? Abstinence or Postponement............................21

Section Two – *The facts of life in the twenty-first century*

Chapter 6
Pregnancy, Abortion, Adoption + All That.........................27

Chapter 7
Birth Control..31

Chapter 8
Sexually Transmitted Infections + HIV.............................35

Chapter 9
Same-Sex Relationships, Sexual Attraction,
Gender + Transgender..41

Chapter 10
Self-Stimulation + Masturbation...................................45

Chapter 11
"Playing Doctor" + Beyond – Childhood Sexual Behavior........49

Section Three – *The first "change of life" – puberty and adolescence*

Chapter 12
Changing Body – Changing Mind..59

Chapter 13
Teens + Sexuality..63

Section Four – *Unavoidable, unfortunate and unsettling outside influences*

Chapter 14
Media + Your Kids...69

Chapter 15
Social Media + Sexting...73

Chapter 16
Pornography..79

Section Five – *The sex talks*

Chapter 17
How to Start + Continue the Conversations.........................87

Chapter 18
The Last + Most Important Things!.......................................95

Chapter 19
Books, Websites and All Kinds of Support!...........................97

References...109

My Story

Thanks so much for purchasing *Birds + Bees + YOUR Kids*. I know how hard it can be to talk about sexuality, love, and relationships with your kids and I'm hopeful I can help you feel more confident and comfortable talking about this part of life. You might worry you'll give your kids too much information or ruin their innocence or blow it in some way you haven't even dreamed up! I feel your pain. Even though I talk about sexuality for a living, I am still uncomfortable talking to my son, but I put on my big girl panties and do it anyway.

Parenting, as you know, is not for wimps.

Throughout my 20's and 30's I provided sexual health education, primarily as a volunteer, for several non-profit organizations in the Seattle area. I worked directly with patients, providing pregnancy, sexually transmitted infections, birth control, and sterilization counseling, and I am also a registered HIV counselor. I discovered that I love talking about sexuality and that I'm darned good at it.

However, when my son had questions about his body and how it works, I was surprised to discover that I was uncomfortable talking to him! I started thinking and realized that if *I* was uncomfortable talking to *my* child, other parents must be even more uncomfortable. Spurred by my own discomfort, I decided to start Birds + Bees + Kids® to help parents become informed, confident, and comfortable talking to their children of any age about sexuality, love, and relationships. I provide parents and caregivers with an environment that encourages them to explore their personal values about this topic and then decide what is right for *their* family based on *their* values.

I live in Seattle and have been married since 1993. When I first wrote this book, our son was nine years-old. He has entered the teen years and you will not be surprised to learn that he is mortified by my work. Despite his discomfort, we push on with the sex talks, rain or shine, and do our darnedest to empower him with piles of information he won't really need until he's in his late 20's – I know, wishful thinking on my part!

Everything you need to know before you start the talks is included here. Once you empowered with this information, whether your kids are 2 or 12, once you complete this guide, you will feel encouraged and inspired to start and then continue the conversations with your kids all through their lives.

Here's to becoming a grandparent on your schedule!

A few words of wisdom about using this book

This guide will feel very much like a personal journey and take you through the process of articulating your values around sexuality, love, and relationships. Just like most journeys, you will have ups and downs as you go along. Go with the flow. And if you need help or support, be sure to reach out a trusted friend or even a therapist. Many people have trauma associated with sexuality and the best and fastest way to feel better is often a little therapeutic tune-up.

- There are questions for you to ponder and I suggest you respond in writing. Go ahead and get a journal to use for this purpose.

- You can use the questions at the end of each section to stimulate discussion with your children's other parent or your friends.

- The process, if done in one sitting, should take about three hours.

- At the end, you will have considerably more clarity about your sexual values and you can use this book to start or continue conversations with your kids.

- Don't be surprised if your values change as your kids get older. This is a process.

- Resources are listed at the end.

SECTION ONE

Your story, beliefs, hopes + dreams

Chapter 1

Sexuality + Values – What Do You Believe?

Sexuality + Values – What Do You Believe?

You know you need to talk to your kids about sex at some point – every parent knows this, right? But where on earth do you start? And how old should your kids be? What if they say they already know everything and won't talk to you at all? What if they ask you how old you were when you first had sex?

Daunting stuff, I know. But before you launch into a discussion of what goes where and why they shouldn't have sex until they're in their mid-thirties and preferably married, there's some work you need to do to make the conversations more effective and go more smoothly. You need to clarify *your* values about sexuality, love, and relationships.

This may sound a little strange because as a child you might have had only one talk with your own nervous parent, who filled you in on the details of reproduction, told you it was for marriage, and said "Feel free to ask me if you have any questions!" and that was the first, last, and only conversation. Or perhaps you learned the "facts" without the values from your friends, a book, or at school. And then, of course, there are those of you who were self-taught and knew intuitively to never ever ask about bodies, love, relationships or, heaven forbid, sexuality or reproduction. Perhaps you looked "sex" up in the dictionary and did the best you could from there.

For most people, your own experience as a child won't do a whole lot to help you when it comes to talking about sex with your own kids. Now with sex everywhere you turn, middle school kids engaging in oral sex, and with HIV and AIDS to worry about, you have a sense of urgency and fear fueling the desire to have open communication with your kids about sex. But you think you don't have the skills to do it "right" or you don't know where or when to start the conversations or even what to say. These concerns are enough to make a person skip the whole conversation and trust your kids' peers and the media to take care of it for you.

4

For many of you, the thought of explaining the mechanics of sex is a big enough deal that it's challenging to move on from there. But, sex is really so much more than just baby making, right? Talking to your kids about sex opens the door to a whole world that, in its entirety, isn't appropriate for your kids to gain access to until they're in their teens.

Starting early and taking the time to have multiple brief conversations is best for everyone. You can figure out what you want your kids to know before they need to know it, and your kids will come to expect this support and information from you. If all goes well, with your guidance, your kids will make great decisions.

This guide is a resource to help you to start clarifying your values so you can effectively influence your children and their sexual decision-making from the very first conversation. According to a 2007 survey of kids age 12 to 17 by the National Campaign to Prevent Teen and Unplanned Pregnancy, parents have the most influence on kids when it comes to making decisions about dating, relationships, and sex.

Most parents think peers have the most influence, probably because of our own experiences growing up. If you think back, maybe it would have been better for you to have been able to talk openly with your parents about these things. Or maybe you were lucky and did. One thing is for sure – our kids are listening to us. They want and need our guidance when it comes to this important part of life.

Parents have the most influence on kids when it comes to making decisions about dating, relationships and sex.

Clarifying your sexual values is one important step on the way to guiding your kids through the tricky world of sexuality, love, and relationships. What do I mean by "sexual values"? Values can be defined as standards or principles with some sort of emotional investment. Sexual values are what you believe to be true for yourself and your family. Your sexual values can be influenced by your religion, your politics, your culture, your experiences, the messages you received from your parents, and your own intuitive sense of what feels right to you.

Talking about the facts and science of sexual reproduction, birth control, Sexually Transmitted Infections (STIs), and HIV with your kids can seem overwhelming, but, lucky for you, there are many great books and websites that can help you provide this information to your kids. You don't need to be an expert on sexual health to guide your kids through discussions about the different aspects of reproduction or HIV transmission. All you really need is a basic understanding and willingness to both initiate conversations and find answers to your kids' questions. And remember, compared to your kids, you are a sex expert!

Talking about your values can be hard because there is no book you can read or website you can visit to tell you what you believe about sexuality, love, and relationships. It's up to you to clarify your values and pass them on to your kids. Some parents have a strong religious background providing clear statements about sex and sexuality. However, if your religion and personal beliefs conflict, it can make it difficult to sort out what you believe.

The idea of waiting until marriage is a perfect example. Teens need compelling reasons to wait to have sex. Just telling them to wait until they are married is probably not reason enough to convince a wildly hormonal teenager to postpone sex. If you don't believe in waiting until marriage for sex, you still need compelling reasons for waiting as long as possible to become sexually active. When you can explain to your child your reasoning behind your beliefs, your child may listen more closely and take time to make smarter decisions. I believe the more thoughtful your responses are to your kids, the more impact they'll have.

When you know what you believe and you've clarified your own values, talking to your children about these things becomes a snap. Well, maybe not a snap, but it'll be easier. You won't fumble around trying to figure out what you believe at the same time your child is looking to you for guidance. Also, the approach you take when you talk to your kids is just as important as what you say. One of the easiest ways to figure out what to say and how to say it is to think about your own experiences as a child or teen and ask "What would have worked better for me?" This can be a great approach to help you talk with your own kids.

If you have young kids, you may find some of the topics and exercises seem too advanced for the age of your children. This guide is to help you plan for the future, and if you take the time now to sort out your beliefs, as your children age, you will find you are well-prepared for these conversations because you've already done at least some of the work.

Also, the sooner you clarify your sexual values and start talking to your kids, the easier it becomes. Starting these conversations when kids are young and continuing them throughout childhood and adolescence helps kids to make better decisions about sexuality, love, and relationships as they grow up. While I can't guarantee that you won't get eye-rolling and sighing from your kids at some point, I can guarantee that *you* will feel more confident and comfortable talking about this subject!

Chapter 2

Your Story – How You Learned about The Birds + The Bees

Your Story – How You Learned about The birds + The Bees

Most people have a memory of learning about sex. No matter how you learned, the experience left some kind of impact - maybe a sense of shame or embarrassment or maybe a sense of wonder and delight. Whatever the impact, it's most likely still with you today and influences how you interact with your kids when it comes to this topic.

One parent told me she asked her mother what "rape" means. Her mother dodged the question, so she looked it up in the dictionary. This led her to the word "sex" and, what do you know, she learned the facts of life - from the dictionary! She also learned her mother wasn't a trustworthy resource and didn't bother to ask her any more questions.

Take a few moments and respond to the following questions to help you think about your experience learning about sexuality, love, and relationships when you were a kid. Describe everything you can remember in detail.

- What are your early memories of learning about sex? Did you learn from your parents, from your siblings or on the playground?

- What were your reactions when you were a kid learning about sex? Reflect on your feelings and your thoughts at the time.

- When you were growing up, what did your religion tell you about sex? What does it say now? Do you agree? Why or why not?

- Describe your parents' relationship(s). Looking back, how healthy do you think they were?

- What did you learn from your parents' relationship(s) that you want to pass on to your children?

- What did you learn that you'd rather not pass on?

- What was the message in your family about same-sex relationships? If your parents are gay or lesbian, how did you feel about this as a child? How did you feel about your family?

- If you learned about sex in school, what do you remember? How was this information helpful?

- If you are a survivor of sexual abuse, how have you come to terms with this? How has this affected your relationship with your child?

The intention of this chapter is to help you understand how your own experiences impact and influence how you parent around sexuality. My hope is you will be more aware of when your personal experiences are showing up and affecting your interactions with your kids.

Chapter 3

Love + Healthy Relationships

Love + Healthy Relationships

If you've been in love at some point in your life, you may recall that it's an exciting, overwhelming, and amazing time! It's important for parents to help kids navigate these crazy, wonderful feelings and make good decisions about their partners. The best way you can help your kids make good relationship choices is to be clear about what you believe the elements of a healthy relationship are and, more importantly, to model this in your own relationships - romantic and otherwise.

As you know from your own life experience, being "in love" as a teen can be very different from of being "in love" as an adult. It's important to be respectful of your teen's relationships and experiences. Allow them to experience love, whatever it looks like, without your judgment and voice of reason. For them, their experience of love is every bit as real and earth-shattering as your grown-up love. Your job is to help your teens to be as healthy and safe in the relationship as possible – not to bring them back to reality. As you well know, the course of the relationship will eventually provide them with plenty of "reality."

Think about healthy, romantic relationships and use a scale of one to five to rate the importance of the following elements. Five equals "very important." Feel free to add any additional elements you think should be included.

Love	1	2	3	4	5
Respect	1	2	3	4	5
Trust	1	2	3	4	5
Commitment	1	2	3	4	5
Maturity	1	2	3	4	5
Communication	1	2	3	4	5
Acceptance	1	2	3	4	5

- In general, what does a healthy romantic relationship look like to you?

- How are you modeling healthy relationships for your children?

- How could you do better?

- Describe an unhealthy romantic relationship.

- What are or will be the rules about dating in your family? What age is it okay to start dating? Will the date have to meet you before they can go out, etc.?

- Who is responsible for setting sexual limits in a relationship and why?

The "SCRIPT!" sections are where you'll find your own way of talking about various issues with your kids. It's best if you actually write these down so you can refer to them later.

SCRIPT! Describe and explain the feeling of sexual desire and what you believe about it.

SCRIPT! What will you tell your child about your hopes for their future healthy romantic relationships and why?

Love and relationships are very likely the most confusing parts of being a teenager. When you are able to talk clearly about your own values and beliefs about relationships, your kids will do better. They really do pay attention to us when we talk about our experiences and even offer occasional advice.

Chapter 4

What Does "Ready for Sex" Mean to You?

What Does "Ready for Sex" Mean to You?

When it comes to sexual decision-making, there are so many different things that can influence the decision to have sex. Read through the list below and think about your own early sexual relationships. Add any influencing factors you believe are missing. How did these play into your sexual decision-making? What did you neglect to consider when you first became sexually active? Some people didn't have a choice about the first time they had sex because they were raped or sexually abused. If this is the case for you, think about the first time you chose to have sex.

Our kids need to have a good understanding of each of these terms and more! They need to know the definition of each word and have an example they can understand. You can start teaching your kids about each of these concepts from an early age, so they have a solid understanding before they're involved in their first relationship. Once they are in middle school, you can then talk to them about how each one of these ideas relates to sexuality and relationships.

Emotional maturity	Curiosity
Pressure	Pleasure
Fun	Guilt
Consequences	Alcohol and drugs
Deliberate decision-making	Waiting
Choice	Temptation
Preparedness	Responsibilty
Agreement and mutuality	Respect
Consent	Communication
Trust	Impulsiveness

Complete the following exercises for each of the terms listed above. You will end up with a big list of mini-scripts!

1) Define each term so a 6-to 8-year-old would understand it.

2) Provide a kid-friendly example from regular life that a 6- to 8-year-old would understand.

3) State how it relates to sex and relationships. You will introduce this concept when your child is around age eleven.

Example – Temptation

Definition: Wanting to do something that may be wrong or you might feel bad about later. You can be tempted to do things you'll feel good about later too.

Example: There are cookies on the kitchen counter. You want to eat one before dinner, but your mom said you can't have one until after dinner.

Sex and Relationships: When you're dating someone and are kissing and fooling around, you may be tempted to have sex. It's important to know that the farther you go, the more you'll be tempted to have sex, maybe before you're ready. What could you do in a situation to help resist the temptation to have sex?

YOUR TURN! Use your journal or a separate piece of paper for this exercise.

Emotional maturity	Curiosity
Pressure	Pleasure
Fun	Guilt
Consequences	Alcohol and drugs
Deliberate decision-making	Waiting
Choice	Temptation
Preparedness	Responsibilty
Agreement and mutuality	Respect
Consent	Communication
Trust	Impulsiveness

Whatever the age of your children, you will probably never be truly ready for them to have sex! By talking about the emotional and social aspects of sexuality and making the decision to become sexually active, your kids will be well ahead of their peers regarding their preparedness. By doing everything you can to help them make good decisions, you'll feel slightly more prepared for this big event.

Chapter 5

Why Wait? Abstinence or Postponement

Why Wait? Abstinence or Postponement

A strong message of abstinence or postponement from parents plus information about birth control, sexually transmitted infections, and HIV really does help kids delay sex. It also increases their use of condoms and birth control. I call this "Abstinence Plus."

Providing information is not the same as giving permission.

Before you develop your own definition of abstinence, you need to define "sex." There is a continuum of physical intimacy from hand holding to kissing to vaginal sex to sexual activities involving multiple partners and who knows what else. Some of these activities are appropriate in public and some in private. The more specific you are in your definitions, the less room there will be for confusion.

- What is your definition of "sex"? Is it just intercourse?

SCRIPT! *What are your core beliefs about sex and relationships? Is it only okay to have sex within a committed relationship? What about "hooking up" or casual sex?*

I know that most parents want their children to wait to have sex until they are "ready" and most of us are never truly ready for our kids to have sex. From my informal polls of parents, it seems that post-high school is the age that parents are comfortable imagining their kids jumping into the world of sexuality, love, and serious relationships.

Some parents want their children to wait until they're married, and while this is a clear event and usually has firm values supporting it, it's important to include the compelling reasons that support the marriage goal. Children who are raised in religious households more often wait to have sex – but not until they are married. Unfortunately, when they do have sex for the first time, they tend to *not* use birth control and condoms.

What if you had sex before marriage but now believe that sex is something reserved for marriage? How do you talk to you kids without feeling like a hypocrite? This is really important: You don't have to reveal your sexual history to your child. You can if you want to, but it isn't required. Just as they have a right to privacy, you do too!

SCRIPT! *Respond to the question, "How old were you when you had sex for the first time?"*

If you don't believe that sex is solely part of a married relationship, explaining reasons to wait to your children can seem challenging. Isn't it easier to just say "Wait until you're married" and leave it at that? Unfortunately, when you say this but don't fully believe it, your kids will eventually figure out that you weren't honest with them. Honesty is an essential part of conversations about this subject.

One way to figure out what "ready for sex" means to you is to consider your own first sexual experiences.

- What was good about your first sexual experiences?

- What was not so good?

- Would you repeat the experience? Why or why not?

SCRIPT! *"I think people should wait to have sex until..." If you believe marriage is the goal, give some good, concrete reason to wait.*

Kids need all the help they can get when it comes to making the decision to wait to have sex. They want and need to hear compelling reasons from you to wait as long as possible and they need to know how to protect themselves so they are prepared when they do have sex.

SECTION TWO

The facts of life in the twenty-first century

Chapter 6

Pregnancy, Abortion, Adoption + All That

Pregnancy, Abortion, Adoption + All That

Unplanned pregnancy is a fact of life, and I think it's safe to say that no parents want their children to experience pregnancy before they're ready. Talking about your beliefs about teen pregnancy, conception, abortion and adoption are some of the most important conversations you can have with your kids.

Conception or fertilization is the moment the egg and sperm connect in the fallopian tube, and pregnancy begins when the fertilized egg implants in the uterine wall.

SCRIPT! *Explain why people give children up for adoption.*

- Do you believe life begins at conception? Why or why not?

- What do you believe about abortion?

- Why do women make the choice to have an abortion?

- What do you think about women who have abortions?

- Do you believe abortion is acceptable only in some circumstances, such as incest or rape? Why or why not?

- How would you feel if your child chose to have an abortion?

- If you know someone who has had an abortion, what do you think about them and their decision?

At least half of American women will experience an unintended pregnancy by age 45, and at current rates about one-third will have had an abortion.

SCRIPT! *Explain abortion to your kids – what it is and your values about it.*

- Imagine your teenager has just confided in you that she thinks she may be pregnant or your son confides that his girlfriend may be pregnant. What is your initial response? Don't bother to "screen" your feelings and thoughts, just let it all out.

- It's probably safe to assume that at least some of what you wrote above isn't going to be particularly helpful to your teenager. What would be helpful to your teen? What would you want to hear if you were in his or her shoes or what did you want to hear if you were in that same situation when you were a teen?

- If your teen, or his girlfriend, has decided to end the pregnancy, what would you say?

- If your teen, or his girlfriend, has decided adoption is the solution to this pregnancy, what could you say?

- What could you say if your teen, or his girlfriend, has decided to keep the baby?

SCRIPT! *What will you say to your children about being a teen parent?*

This exercise is intended to get you thinking about teen pregnancy and your beliefs about it, so you can find ways to talk about it in a thoughtful way. If your child does become pregnant or impregnates someone, your reaction may surprise you, but if you have already been talking about your beliefs and values, your reaction may not be a surprise to your teen. This may help pave the way for an easier conversation about the situation, should it arise. And hopefully it won't!

Chapter 7

Birth Control

Birth Control

The only form of birth control that is 100% effective is abstinence. While there are many other forms of birth control, this is the only method guaranteed to work effectively every time it's used. Unfortunately, practicing abstinence is really hard to do when your hormones are raging. Most of us have been there, and even as adults we've probably made choices that weren't the smartest when it came to pregnancy and STI protection.

The problem with abstinence is when it fails, it fails miserably. Most research is showing kids want and need to know about birth control, even if you strongly believe sex is reserved only for marriage and have made this very clear to your kids. In fact, what works best for kids is a strong message of abstinence plus information about birth control and STIs.

Providing information about birth control is not the same as giving permission to use it. It's just smart, because I don't think there is a parent out there who would wish an unplanned pregnancy on their teenaged kid. I am hopeful that you would rather be really angry and disappointed in your children's choices rather than deal with an unplanned pregnancy.

I'm not going to discuss every method of birth control – you can easily find that information from a variety of sources. I want you to explore your beliefs about birth control and how you will talk to your kids about it.

Finally, in this time of HIV and AIDS kids need to know when they have sex, they should use a condom every time – even if they are using another form of birth control. Other than abstinence, condoms are the best way to prevent the transmission of STIs and HIV. If this works for your family, when you say sex -- say condom. The two should go together like bread and butter.

When you say "sex" – say condom!

SCRIPT! Explain what birth control is and why it's used.

The following are some statements intended to help you further clarify your values about birth control.

My religion says using birth control is **good/bad/neutral/don't know** ... and I **agree/disagree** with this because...

I want my daughter to be protected from pregnancy. **True/False**

I believe birth control is morally wrong. **True/False**

I will help my daughter get birth control before she needs it. **True/False**

I will make sure my kids know about and understand how to use every form of birth control that's currently available. **True/False**

I will have condoms available in my home for my children to use, no questions asked. **True/False**

I will take my children to get birth control if they ask me to. **True/False**

I will make sure my children know where to get birth control if they need it. **True/False**

- Is there anything else you want your kids to know about birth control?

- What will you do if you find out your child is sexually active and NOT using birth control?

- What will you do if you suspect your child is sexually active, but you don't believe in using birth control?

When kids have information about birth control, their risk of unplanned pregnancy goes down. Just because children have information about birth control it doesn't mean they think they now have permission to have sex. It just means they are more likely to use it when they become sexually active.

Chapter 8

Sexually Transmitted Infections + HIV

Sexually Transmitted Infections (STI) + HIV

In this day and age of HIV and AIDS, we must talk to our kids about sexually transmitted infections and sooner than we think! If you watch the news or listen to the radio when your kids are around, they have most likely heard the words and possibly engaged in discussion with friends about AIDS. If your child has started puberty, he or she should know that people can sometimes pass germs and can become very sick from having sex. Perhaps this will act as a deterrent to sexual activity! Every little nudge towards waiting to have sex is a good one, right?

You don't need to know every little detail of each infection, but it's helpful to have a basic understanding of symptoms and methods of transmission. The Centers for Disease Control website is a good place to start if you need more information. Check the resources section for more information.

Remember! The best way to prevent an STI or HIV is to abstain from sex of any kind – oral, anal, and vaginal. The second best way is to encourage kids to use a condom every time they have sex. Finally, long-term monogamy with an honest and faithful partner is also very effective. Considering most people have sex at age 17 and then don't get married until their late 20's, it's safer to be frank and very clear about your expectations about condom use.

These statistics are from the Office of Adolescent Health:

- Adolescents ages 15-24 account for nearly half of the 20 million new cases of STI's each year.

- Today, four in 10 sexually active teen girls have had an STI that can cause infertility and even death.

Also, though rates of HIV are very low among adolescents, males make up more than two-thirds of HIV diagnoses among 13- to 19-year-olds.

SCRIPT! *Write a simple explanation of what an STI is and how to prevent its spread.*

I'm going to make it a little easier and provide a simple starter script for discussing HIV and AIDS. This is vitally important information for your children to have, and it's important that the information you give them is accurate. It's best to have this conversation by about age 10.

"There is a Sexually Transmitted Infection called HIV that causes an illness called AIDS. It's caused by a virus or germ that travels from person to person in body fluids – blood, semen, vaginal secretions, and breast milk.

The HIV virus eats away at the immune system that usually keeps us healthy. The white blood cells can't fight off regular illnesses and diseases, and a person with HIV eventually develops AIDS.

It's sad because AIDS causes the person to die. There is no cure right now, but people can take medicines that help them to be healthy and live as long as possible.

Having sexual intercourse with an infected partner is one way to get HIV. This means vaginal, anal, or oral sex. You can also get HIV from sharing needles to inject drugs.

The best way to prevent HIV infection is to not have sex and not use intravenous drugs. If you decide to have sex, using a condom every time can stop you from becoming infected with HIV. Also, having one partner w ho does not have sex with other people can prevent HIV."

This is just to get you started. The Sexuality Information and Education Council of the United States provides excellent information about how to talk to kids of all ages about HIV and AIDS. Check the resources section for more information.

SCRIPT! Explain what a condom is, how it's used and why to use one.

Safer sex means sexual activity that does not involve any exchange of body fluids – semen, vaginal secretions, blood, or breast milk. Kissing, touching, sexual talk, sex with a condom, and sex within a mutually monogamous relationship are examples of safer sex activities.

SCRIPT! What will you say to reassure your kids about deciding to have sex and the possibility of contracting an STI or becoming pregnant?

Do you know anyone who has HIV or AIDS? What do you think about them and their circumstances?

- There is vaccine available for the Human Papillomavirus (HPV), an STI that causes cervical, mouth, throat and anal cancers. In order for it to be effective, it needs to be given before people become sexually active, by about age 11. What do you think about this vaccine? Would you give it to your child? Why or why not?

- What will you say to your child if they confide in you that they have contracted an STI?

Sexually Transmitted Infections, HIV, and AIDS can be really scary to think about; especially when you think about the risks you know teenagers take. Thinking about talking to your younger child about STIs and HIV is also a frightening prospect. Remember, when you provide this information in a loving, supportive, non-threatening way, your kids will be considerably less frightened than if they learn through misinformation from their peers.

Chapter 9

Same-Sex Relationships, Sexual Attraction, Gender + Transgender

Same-Sex Relationships, Sexual Attraction, Gender + Transgender

Same-sex relationships and sexual attraction are a part of life, and it's important you talk to your kids about them. Whether you believe being gay is totally and completely fine or totally and completely wrong or somewhere in between, it's important for children to know about same-sex relationships and sexual attraction. If you are a gay or lesbian parent, then you know how important and impactful parents' reactions to this can be. I believe kids need to know about sexual attraction and how it's possible to be attracted to someone who is the same sex, opposite sex or both. Most kids want to know they are normal and it's our job to help them with this.

Sexual attraction means whom you are sexually and romantically attracted to - someone of the same sex, opposite sex, or both.

A word of caution – because you can't tell by looking if a person is gay or lesbian (and this includes your own kids), it's important to discuss this topic with care and sensitivity, no matter what you believe. If your child is gay and you believe this is wrong, the last thing your child needs is to think you will hate him or her because of this. Most gay people will tell you that their attraction to the opposite sex is not a choice.

The most important thing when discussing this issue is to remain in communication with your child. Gay teens have a higher rate of suicide, and open communication and support from you can make this very personal and sometimes difficult discovery easier. As you can imagine, it is difficult to be gay in our culture, and the more supportive you can be to your kid, the better off the child will be.

As part of natural and healthy sexual behavior, sometimes kids engage in role-playing games involving some sexual experimentation, usually between the ages of 6 and 12. Two girls playing a game of "wedding" need someone to be the groom. If the game progresses to the honeymoon night, some experimentation can occur. Because the girls are the same sex, this does not make either or both of them gay. It's most likely a matter of availability.

- What was the message growing up in your family about being gay or lesbian?

- f you are a gay or lesbian parent, what are your particular parenting challenges or concerns?

- What do you remember about learning what it means to be gay or lesbian?

- How will you talk about gay and/or lesbian sex?

SCRIPT! *Explain what gay means and your beliefs about same-sex relationships.*

SCRIPT! *What will you say to your child if you think they are gay or lesbian?*

Sometimes people are born into the wrong body for their gender. This is called being transgender. Our gender identity is an intrinsic part of how we see ourselves; who we identify with in terms of interests, feelings, social roles and connection – boys or girls, men or women. Most people feel at home in their male or female body and their gender identity matches their physical body.

- Do you know anyone who is transgender? What do you think about them and their unique gender identity?

- What do you think it's important to tell kids about transgender people?

- If you don't understand being gay, lesbian, bi or transgender, what can you do to learn more about these ways of being?

Considering the world we live in, even your very young child can understand why their friend has two mommies or daddies. Introducing the idea of same-sex relationships, transgender people, and your values early helps kids make sense of the world.

Chapter 10

Self-Stimulation + Masturbation

Self-Stimulation + Masturbation

What an amazing thing, the human body! Our kids think they are pretty amazing too, and once they figure out that it feels good when they touch their penis or clitoris – watch out! Kids under 5 will touch their privates whenever and wherever. If it feels good, why not do it?

Babies and young children "self-stimulate" – it just feels good to touch their privates, and they usually do this to relieve stress and to self-soothe. Masturbation involves fantasy and more adult-like thinking when touching privates. It's important for kids to know that it's normal to masturbate and also normal not to masturbate. If self-stimulation or masturbation involves others, is interrupting regular play, or becomes a central activity, it might be time to talk to a professional.

How we react when young kids self-stimulate is very important. Because we want them to know we are trustworthy and safe to talk to about bodies, sexuality and, well, anything, it's really important to remain calm, cool, and collected when this is going on. This means no yelling, shaming, or blaming, even if you believe self-stimulation and masturbation are always inappropriate.

If we yell at kids when they are engaged in any kind of "sexual behavior," especially young children, they interpret our reaction to mean we can't handle this kind of behavior, so they may begin to sneak and hide the behavior. They will make an effort to keep us from being upset by hiding these behaviors. If your child thinks you will freak out about any behavior involving their privates, it could mean your child won't tell you if something really scary is happening to them.

We can teach them in a loving way that this is something people do in private and alone. It's important to say "alone" because little kids think being at home on the couch watching TV is private. Just calmly redirect their behavior and let them know it's fine to touch their privates, but it's something people do in private, alone.

- What was the message you received in childhood about self-stimulation and masturbation?

- What are your beliefs about it now?

SCRIPT! *Write a statement about self-stimulation and masturbation that includes a message about privacy and your beliefs.*

Most of us are pretty uncomfortable when it comes to talking about masturbation. It's one of those things that pretty much everybody does and no one talks about. Openness about this topic can help your kids to feel "normal" – something every kid worries about at one time or another.

Chapter 11

"Playing Doctor" + Beyond – Childhood Sexual Behavior

"Playing Doctor" + Beyond – Childhood Sexual Behavior

General Childhood Sexual Development

Kids are naturally curious about their own bodies and each other's. After all, what could be more interesting than a penis if you don't have one or have never seen one? A certain amount of "playing doctor" or body exploration is perfectly typical and natural throughout childhood.

Parents of preschoolers get to hear a lot of potty talk, questions about pregnancy and birth, and conversations and comments relating to differences in body parts. Showing and looking at private body parts and self-stimulation in public and private are also part of the fun. Occasionally kids will touch each other's privates, usually out of curiosity, not because they are trying to sexually stimulate in some way.

All of the above is developmentally normal, and just because it's natural and healthy, doesn't mean we have to be comfortable with it. However, as parents who want their children to be comfortable talking to us about any and everything, we need to be careful about monitoring our sometimes-strong reactions to their typical sexual curiosity and development.

Sometimes this behavior can cross the line and become "sexualized" which means, essentially, it's adult-like. Usually the child is imitating something they have seen or that they have physically experienced themselves. This behavior is not typical and healthy, and I would recommend close monitoring and consultation with a professional as it can indicate sexual abuse. Not always, however, so don't immediately assume the worst.

Natural and healthy sexual play is *spontaneous, mutual, and good-humored.* It spontaneously emerges out of play and looks like play; both kids agree to play this way without threats or coercion; and they are having fun. This is a quick and easy way for you to determine how much you need to worry about the behavior.

When to worry: Imitating adults sexually (sexualized play); sex play using force, threats, dominance, violence, aggression; and/or compulsiveness. Remember, children who are engaging in sexualized play may need help, and their parents should be contacted.

One of the most important ways for you to determine just how concerned you should be is your intuition. If you have that "uh-oh" or gut feeling that something is wrong, 9 times out of 10, you will be right. Trust your gut – it is your ally.

Children continue to explore each other's bodies throughout their childhood and adolescence. As elementary age kids, this usually takes the form of role-playing games and some mild experimentation. As kids enter puberty, usually around 11 or so, their exploration becomes a little more adult-like, including kissing, body rubbing, and rarely, actual intercourse.

Once they are solidly into puberty, a child's sexual behavior, curiosity and interest usually increases and becomes more and more adult-like. In fact, the sexual behavior of 13 to 16 year-olds often looks just like adult sexual behavior. Parents find this troubling and confusing, especially since most teens are really not ready for the ins and outs of a full sexual relationship. Their blossoming bodies are years ahead of their hearts and minds when it comes to sex and relationships.

No matter their age, kids need information about okay touch and not okay touch and regular reminders about keeping their bodies safe. They need to know that they are the "boss" of their body and have the right to say no to any kind of play, or touch, sexual or otherwise. Young kids also need to know about reproductive biology because it gives them a reference point for sexual activity, i.e., it's not for kids.

If we yell at kids when they are engaged in any kind of "sexual behavior," especially young children, they learn that we can't handle this kind of behavior, so it may go underground. They will make an effort to keep us from being upset. This could mean your child won't tell you if something really scary is happening, like someone is sexually abusing them.

It's pretty much safe to say most parents are terrified their child will be sexually abused. Part of this fear comes from our own experiences and part from the number of stories we hear in the news, on TV, and the internet about "stranger danger," sexual abuse, exploitation, and abduction. It seems like a potential abuser is lurking on every corner.

Sadly, the majority of sexual abusers are known to the child, and the idea of "stranger danger" is bunk. Make sure your kids know they can tell you if something uncomfortable or bad happens to them. They need to hear that you are available to them. And more than that, they need to see it.

This means not freaking out when they are "playing doctor" or touching their privates. When you remain calm in these moments, our kids learn we can handle this kind of body stuff. When we freak out, they learn that we can't handle it, and the behavior can go underground.

When kids know about sexual intercourse, they are safer. Sexual predators look for kids who are "innocent" and don't have open relationships with their parents.

Besides not freaking out, the best thing you can do for your kids is to teach them from an early age they are the boss of their bodies. They have the right to say no (and loudly) if someone touches them in a way they don't like or feels uncomfortable. Of course there are times when you or a doctor or nurse will need to touch their penis or vulva, but make sure they understand this is for a reason – they are hurting or sick or just to make sure everything is fine.

When our kids have clear boundaries, know words to use, and have loving, open parents, they are safer. When they know about sexuality, how babies are made, the names of their private body parts (penis, scrotum, vulva and vagina), and that sex is not for kids, they are safer. And when they are older and can talk to you about the tricky world of sexuality and sexual feelings, they are safer.

Here is a simple script you can use with your kids when they are engaging in any type of sexual play – even if you catch your teenager in the living room having sex!

Your tone should be calm – even if you are completely freaked out – because you want your kids to know you can handle anything that comes your way. No yelling, shaming, blaming, or being big and scary (if you can help it!).

You may need to repeat the steps a few times with the kids before they get fully redirected from this behavior. If the behavior is adult-like in any way, or if it just isn't stopping, I'd recommend you contact one of the resources at the end of the book for more help.

Step 1: Describe the behavior -- "I see you and Billy are looking at each other's penises."

Step 2: Describe your reaction -- "I feel uncomfortable when this happens."

Step 3: Redirect -- "Pull up your pants and let's go play outside."

Step 4: Regroup – Ask yourself, "What just happened here? What is my intuition telling me?"

Step 5: Plan – Ask yourself, "What do I need to do next?" This step always includes telling the other parent the kids were "playing doctor." Depending on the behavior, it may include a call to child protective services.

If the behavior continues, start with "I've told you this before..." and between Step 1 and 2 add "This needs to stop." Be clear, kind and firm, but not mean or threatening.

This script really will work for kids of any age – just substitute "making out on the couch" for "looking at each other's penises" and you are good to go. Remember to stay calm, cool, and collected and you'll be able to manage yourself and the situation with grace.

Don't feel bad if the information in this chapter is new to you or if you've yelled at your kids when they have been exploring. Most of our personal experience around sexual behavior wasn't positive, so we aren't well-prepared to handle this behavior by our own kids. If you were sexually abused, these behaviors can be even more challenging for you, and it's very important for your mental health and your relationship with your children for you to get some help if you haven't already. Connect with the good people at RAINN.org for therapy referrals.

SECTION THREE

The first "change of life" – pubertyand adolescence

Chapter 12

Changing Body – Changing Mind

Changing Body – Changing Mind

We all have memories of when our bodies began to go through the process of puberty – physically changing from a child to an adult, and adolescence – psychologically changing to an adult. Maybe you found this to be an exciting time or maybe it was confusing to you. Perhaps you had a book explaining the process or you watched a film at school while separated from the opposite sex.

Or maybe you had no information at all and were surprised to discover that you were bleeding "down there" for no good reason. Or perhaps you had a wet dream and had no idea what was going on. Whatever your experience, good, bad or ugly, it will probably impact your experience of your child's changing body and changing mind.

When she started to develop breasts, a woman I know thought she had breast cancer because she felt the lump of the mammary gland and breast tissue. No one told her this was normal, and she didn't have anyone to ask!

- When and how did you learn about the changes of puberty?

- Write down some of your earliest memories of your changing body.

- Was there anything that confused or scared you?

- How did your parents react when you began puberty?

- What do you remember about your emotional state at this time?

- What did you want to hear from your parents about this time in your life?

- What do you think about your child physically and emotionally becoming a man or woman? Are you looking forward to these changes? Why or why not?

SCRIPT! *If you're a mom, tell the story of your first period. If you are a dad, talk about how you managed those pesky spontaneous erections and/or your first wet dream!*

SCRIPT! *What is the most important thing you want your child to know about puberty and adolescence? "I want you to know... because..."*

Puberty and adolescence is a challenging time for both parents and kids. The more you can prepare yourself for this change of life, the better, and remember – they are just as baffled by the changes in their body, mind, and attitude as you may be.

Chapter 13

Teens + Sexuality

Teens + Sexuality

Teens have sex, and most of us did too, whether we were ready for it or not. As adults and parents, we have thoughts and judgments about sexually active teens that have probably changed since we were teens ourselves. Remember, if you have young kids, you will be getting a jump on the game by exploring these questions.

Slightly more than one-half of adolescents have engaged in heterosexual oral sex. In fact, higher proportions of teens have engaged in this activity than have engaged in vaginal sex.

Spend some time thinking about your beliefs about teenagers and sex and go deeper than one-word answers.

- How do you feel about your teen having sex?

- How do you feel about teens using birth control without their parents' knowledge?

- What do you think about girls who offer oral sex to boys they barely know?

- What do you think about boys who accept offers of oral sex from girls they barely know?

- How do you feel about teenagers who are sexually active but don't use birth control?

- How would you feel if your teen contracted a sexually transmitted infection? What would you do?

- What do you think about parents who allow their kids to have sex in their home? Would you?

Consider "should" or "should not":

1) Teenagers **should/should not** be allowed to have sex in their own home.

2) Teenagers **should/should not** masturbate.

3) Teenagers **should/should not** be able to get birth control without parental consent.

4) Teenagers **should/should not** be able to get STI and HIV testing without parental consent.

5) Teenagers **should/should not** be able to terminate a pregnancy without parental consent.

6) Teenagers **should/should not** date people three or more years older than they are.

7) Teenagers **should/should not** become parents.

When you know what you believe about teen sexuality, have thought about it, talked with our friends and family about it, you'll feel better about your own teen's sexuality. If your kids are young and you are wondering how this is helpful to you now, remember – you have a jump on the game. You won't have to do this work in the heat of the moment because you know what your values are now.

SECTION FOUR

Unavoidable, unfortunate and unsettling outside influences

Chapter 14

Media + Your Kids

Media + Your Kids

Our kids are bombarded with media messages wherever they go, and most of the media exposure is at home, in front of their own televisions. Kids in the U.S. watch an average of four hours of television every day. According to a study by the Kaiser Family Foundation, 70% of all television programs have some content related to sex – characters talk about it, joke about it, or engage in it.

Because most of us don't watch every moment of TV with our kids, this means they're bombarded with messages about sexuality, love, and relationships consistently but without our values attached to these messages. They're learning what it means to be a boy or a girl, how to talk to the opposite sex, values about dating, marriage, and, on very rare occasions, how to practice safer sex.

Our kids are also learning which products to buy and how to dress. For girls this is particularly challenging, because they're exposed to messages about sexuality at a very early age, and because of this, young girls can start dressing and behaving like teenagers. Perhaps you've noticed young girls dressing like teenagers in low-slung jeans, midriff-baring tops, and high heeled boots. This is an example of the sexualization of young girls; they look and dress in a manner beyond their years. It can be very confusing for girls, especially if they attract attention of a sexual nature before they are prepared to deal with it.

Our boys are not immune to this phenomenon. They are watching the girls in their classes and learning, right along with them, what it means to be valuable as a girl or woman in our culture. I can't help but wonder what they are thinking and deciding about girls when they see them dressed in provocative clothing. Boys also learn that "getting" sex is an important goal, and this idea is presented to them repeatedly in the media.

It's important we talk about these messages our kids so we can help them navigate our increasingly confusing world. When they are able to understand that what they see on TV and in movies isn't reality, we equip them to make better choices.

Except for sleeping, children ages 8 to 18, spend more time in front of computer, television, and game screens than any other activity. This is as much time as the average adult spends at work.

- What kind of media are your kids exposed to - TV shows, video games, song lyrics and movies?

- What do you think your kids are learning from these shows?

- What are three things you could discuss with your children after viewing sexual content on TV or after watching a music video?

- What are your family rules about television viewing? If you don't have any, make some up!

- What are your family rules about clothing? If you don't have any, make some up!

SCRIPT! What does "sexy" mean? How would you explain this to your child? Remember! Three quarters of the word is "SEX!"

SCRIPT! *What do you want your kids to know about how media influences their decision-making?*

Media and its influence are nearly impossible to avoid. Even if you restrict screen time, your kids will be exposed to all sorts of things. It's not your fault. Read *So Sexy, So Soon – The New Sexualized Childhood and What Parents Can Do to Protect Their Kids* for more information and support about this topic. It's in the resources section.

Chapter 15

Social Media + Sexting

Social Media + Sexting

Parents often have a hard time understanding the modern teen world of constant texting, chatting, posting and online communication. Teens are so over-scheduled these days, they barely have time to socialize live-and-in-person like we did. Many find time at the end of the day, late at night after the house is asleep, and spend hours on social media "connecting" with their friends.

Sometimes they post overtly sexual pictures or statements on social media sites and this can put them at risk for predatory behavior, bullying, teasing, and sexual harassment. We have all heard terrible stories of bullying that lead to a child's isolation, depression and suicide.

Social media is not a good replacement for in-person, peer-to-peer communication and socializing. If your child spends more time with his or her friends online than in real life, it's time to make a change so they can connect with their friends and learn how to have real relationships.

- How much are you engaging in social media? What are you communicating to your children about social media and its role in life?

- At what age will you allow your child to use social media?

- How comfortable are you keeping tabs on your child's social media use? Is this something you do (or will do?)? Why or why not?

- What are your family rules about computer/screen use?

Sexting

Tons of teens send sexually provocative photographs – "sexting." Most teens consider this a normal and expected part of modern teen life. Unless a photograph is broadcast widely and embarrassingly, it's usually not big deal. As adults, most of us find this baffling - why on earth would a girl send a picture of her breasts to a boy she barely knows? Or a boy a picture of his penis to his girlfriend?

I see sexting as a natural and normal extension of natural and normal teen sexuality. The reasons they do this are fairly simple – impulsivity, pressure (sometimes), a sense of safety (it's sexy, but not sex), following the pack and a natural urge to express and experience sexuality. This combination is a pressure cooker of potential trouble. Teens have always wanted and needed to express their sexuality and they have always managed to do this in safe and not-so-safe ways.

Take a step back and consider sexting from their perspective. Say a boy wants to get closer to a girl and he has sexual and romantic feelings for her. Way back when in the 1980s or even '90s, he would have been able to chat with her in person, go to a school dance, hang out after school some, meet up at the mall and flirt, flirt, flirt. Maybe even sneak in some hand holding, kissing and *gasp* make out or have sex.

Because it isn't so easy for kids to get together anymore, and because communicating via text has become the standard, any flirting and typical sexual behavior happens through texting. Add on the assumed "privacy" and what you get is a photo of this boy's penis sent to his intended. Think about this as though everything is turned up to maximum volume, but no one is wearing ear plugs because they don't think they need them.

Aside from the fact that most girls never want to see a picture of a boy's penis, the biggest problem is when any sexually graphic picture of a minor is transmitted it's considered trafficking child pornography – a felony. It's also a felony to possess the image and to create it. Triple whammy. The laws vary from state to state, but most have not caught up to the technology and kids can get into a lot of trouble for an impulsive moment.

Even though sexting can be seen as a now-typical behavior in teens, it doesn't mean it's okay. It's very important to talk to your kids about the dangers of sexting and to help them have a plan in place if and when they receive an unwanted text. They also need to know they can talk to you if they make a mistake and send one. Your job is to be an advocate for your child, even when they screw up.

How would you explain the risks of texting these types of photos? Consider both the emotional and legal consequences.

- What would motivate a boy to send a picture of his privates to a girl?

- What would motivate a girl to send a nude picture to a boy?

- What would you do if you discovered your child had sent a sext? Received one?

SCRIPT! *What do you want your kids to know about the risks of sexting?*

SCRIPT! *How will you coach your kids to respond to inappropriate texting?*

Teen life has become so inundated with sexual messages and behavior it's very hard to avoid. I think this is a blessing because it means there are nearly endless opportunities for sex talks!

Chapter 16

Pornography

Pornography

These days, we can't talk about pornography without talking about the internet. The two are forever linked, and now porn is accessible without even trying to find it. Pornographers don't care about your child or your values. They want to hook people – no matter their age – so they can make money. Gone are the days of sneaking peeks at somebody's father's *Playboy* magazine and worrying about getting caught.

It has become important to have explicit conversations with our kids about pornography by approximately age 9, because it is so easy to find, and it can be highly addictive. And this is very close to the average age most kids see it for the first time. They need to know what it is and your beliefs and values about it, especially as it relates to kids. They need to know what to do when they encounter it accidentally or when friends show them porn sites.

The internet is the crack cocaine of pornography – easy to get and highly addictive.

You also need to control access to your computer. This means having the computer in a public place, using parental controls to ensure your child doesn't accidentally (or purposefully) look at porn sites. You need to check your child's history on the computer and discuss internet safety regularly. It's possible to go from looking for "big boobies" to bestiality in a few keystrokes.

Viewing sexually explicit imagery before a person is psychologically ready can be confusing, stimulating and scary – possibly creating the opposite of a healthy relationship with sex and sexuality. Because the teen brain is still developing, I believe explicit sexual imagery can do more harm than good. It can set up unrealistic expectations about sex and make real sexual encounters confusing and less appealing.

After you finish this book or this section of the book, please take some time to learn about pornography and its influence on our relationships, culture, women, men, and families. Check the resources section for some great books and websites.

Pornography is sexually explicit pictures, film, writing, or other material, and the primary purpose is to cause sexual arousal.

SCRIPT! *Explain "sexually explicit" to your child.*

- What was your first experience looking at pornography?

- What do you remember thinking and/or feeling when you looked at porn for the first time?

- What is your current relationship with pornography? What do you think about it now?

- Do you believe viewing pornography is healthy? Why or why not?

- Why do some people find pornography appealing?

- How do you think pornography affects:

  Men -

  Women -

  Children -

  Teenagers -

  Relationships -

- How do you think pornography impacts people's expectations about sex and sexual relationships?

- Viewing porn can feel good to teens. What are few other ways teens can deal with their sexual feelings?

- What are some of your family rules about the internet? If you don't have any, make some up!

- Explain why you have these rules.

SCRIPT! Provide a script for your children to use if someone shows them pornography on a computer or smartphone. And this WILL happen to your child.

Whatever you believe about pornography, it's important to talk about it and talk about safe use of the internet on a regular basis. Kids need to be reminded of our values and beliefs – they forget!

SECTION FIVE

The sex talks

Chapter 17

How to Start + Continue the Conversations

How to start and continue the conversations

If you have yet to start the conversation, it's most likely time to start. If you have been talking to your kids for a while, but haven't been thoughtfully including your values in the conversations, now you can!

Kids are ready and able to learn the basics of reproduction at about age five or six. I know, I know, this seems young! There are several reasons why I believe starting the conversation so early is beneficial.

1) They're usually entering kindergarten and will be meeting and interacting with all kinds of kids who have all kinds of information. Your child needs to have the necessary information from you because you're a trustworthy source, unlike an older child on the playground.

2) They're blank slates. They don't know what we know about sexuality, love, and relationships. They don't know to be embarrassed or ashamed. They don't know what it means to be in a sexual relationship. Ideally, they don't know about rape, porn, or sexual abuse. They learn about sex like anything else they're interested in - such as volcanoes or horses – with openness and curiosity.

3) Kids who know about sex are offered some protection from sexual abuse. Child molesters look for children who are "innocent." When children know sex is *not* for kids, because you've told them so, there's a higher likelihood they'll resist the behavior and be more likely to tell you if it happens.

4) Starting age-appropriate conversations early makes more involved conversations about this subject much easier for you later on. Talking about the facts of reproduction, puberty, STIs, and HIV with your young kid is much easier than talking to your "madly in love" 14-year-old about waiting to have sex. Starting the conversations at a young age gives you many years of practice before adolescence.

Tips for Starting the Conversation

- Get a book. Read with your children if they're under the age of seven. If they're older, they may not be willing to read with you. Be sure to read the book yourself before you hand it off to your kids. Your kid will eventually read the book – there isn't a kid on the planet that doesn't have questions. See the resources page for age-appropriate book suggestions.

- Don't make a big event out of it! Throw a book in with the regular nightly reading; bring it up in the car as you are headed to the grocery store or as you are tucking them in at night.

- Take advantage of "teachable moments." Pregnant friends, teachers, celebrities, TV and movies, their friends who date, and HIV and AIDS in the news can all be catalysts for conversations with your kids.

- Don't wait for your child to ask you about sex. It's your job to initiate these conversations! When you wait for them to ask, you're making them responsible for their sexual health education. This isn't their job – it's yours (for better or worse!).

- Apologize to your older (9+) kids for not talking to them sooner. Say "I'm sorry we haven't talked about this before. I feel a little uncomfortable, and you might, too, but this is important stuff, so we'll be talking about it from now on."

- Be brave and ask your older kids what they know or remember about baby making, stages of puberty, or STIs and HIV. This is a great way to get the conversation started with older kids.

- Divide the labor. If you are comfortable talking about sex, STIs, and HIV, all the scientific stuff, and your spouse isn't, make dating and relationships his or her responsibility.

- Script answers to the topics you are most terrified of discussing. You might have covered some of them here, but make sure you have your top 5-10 ready to go.

Tips for Continuing the Conversations

- Remember, this isn't one long conversation. It is a series of short and sweet conversations throughout childhood and adolescence.

- Give "Public Service Announcements" as you are driving. Remind your kids of your values as you head to the grocery store. Be funny about it, not preachy – they will listen to you.

- Plan what you will say before you say it. Make a script and practice when you're alone in your car. Scripts aren't cheating – they're smart!

- If your kids are unwilling to talk to you, tell them you need two minutes of their time and have them time you. Then tell your kids what you want them to know. If they don't stop you from talking, don't go over five minutes because you don't want them to be overwhelmed with information.

- You don't have to know everything – just be willing to find out the answers when you don't know and willing to talk to your kids.

- Don't worry about providing too much information. Well-meaning parents really can't do much damage to their kids. Try to keep the conversations age-appropriate and trust your instincts. No one will die if your seven-year-old knows about condoms.

- Repeat yourself. Kids don't remember every little detail, so it's your job to give them the same information several times throughout their childhood and adolescence.

- Ask open ended questions like, "What do you think about the kids you know who are having sex?" or "When do you think it's an okay time to become sexually active?" or "What do you think 'sexy' means?"

- Talk about what you remember about having crushes, your first boy- or girlfriend, your friend's relationships, and dating. They like to hear our stories.

- Make sure your kids have a trustworthy adult they can confide in that isn't you (or your partner/spouse.) This could be your sister, brother, best friend, or anyone who shares your values. Chances are good they will come to this adult first to test the waters.

- Finally, relax! You can handle these conversations and the payoff can be huge.

Chapter 18

The Last and Most Important Things!

The last and most important things!

These last two questions are my absolute favorites. Take some time to think them through and be as detailed and thoughtful as possible.

- When you think about sexuality, love, and relationships, what are your hopes for your child?

- When you think about talking to your child about sexuality, love, and relationships, what are your hopes for yourself?

I encourage you to keep your focus on your hopes, rather than our cultural messages, your experiences as a kid, and what the neighbors might think. You will serve your kids well if you know and talk about your hopes and expectations for their future.

When you talk to your kids about your sexual values, you teach them how to communicate, manage themselves under pressure and use good decision-making skills. These gifts will last a lifetime and serve them in a variety of situations, not just where sex is concerned. If you can talk to your kids about sex, you can talk to them about anything! And if you can talk to your kids about anything, chances are good your kids will make better choices and lead happier, healthier lives.

And who wouldn't want that?

Chapter 19

Books, Websites + All Kinds of Support!

Recommended reading for kids

For ages 3 to 8

It's MY Body – A Book to Teach Young Children How to Resist Uncomfortable Touch

Lory Freeman

This simple book for young children provides straightforward scenarios and scripts for kids to use for how to deal with uncomfortable touch. A classic book by Parenting Press.

What's the Big Secret? Talking about Sex with Girls and Boys

Laurie Krasny Brown, Ed.D. and Mark Brown

This book for young children introduces the basics of body differences, baby making, pregnancy, birth, and good and bad touches. It's thoughtfully written and illustrated by the creator of *Arthur* and his spouse.

It's Not The Stork! A Book About Girls, Boys, Babies, Bodies, Families

Robie Harris and Michael Emberley

This is a great book for kids 2 to 5. It has great comic-book-style illustrations and the perfect amount of information about bodies, babies, pregnancy, birth, friendships, different kinds of families, keeping safe and love. A great place to start them off on a positive note!

It's So Amazing! A Book about Eggs, Sperm, Birth, Babies and Families

Robie Harris and Michael Emberley

This is my all-time favorite book about sex, for kids 5 to 11. It has great comic-book-style illustrations and detailed information about pregnancy, birth, sex, bodies, families, keeping safe, HIV, and love. Your kids will refer back to this book over and over again.

Red: A Crayon's Story

Michael Hall

This lovely book for young children helps them understand that sometimes someone will look like a certain kind of person on the outside, but feel like a different kind of person on the inside.

For ages 8 and older

The Care & Keeping of You: The Body Book for Girls (American Girl Library)

Valerie Schaefer

A great guide for girls about their bodies and all the changes of puberty – including information about nutrition, sports safety, feelings, and how to insert a tampon. It's one of several wonderful *American Girl Library* social issue books.

The Girls Body Book: Everything You Need to Know for Growing Up YOU!

Kelli Dunham

This book, for girls only, is a smarter version of *The Care & Keeping of You*. Helpful comments from real girls, as well as inspirational quotes throughout, help make this one a winner.

The Boy's Body Book: Everything You Need to Know for Growing Up YOU!

Kelli Dunham and Steven Bjorkman

The go-to guide for boys about their bodies and the changes of puberty, this book discusses skin, hair, family relationships, friendships, and wet dreams. This book offers advice and support for boys only.

I Am Jazz

Jessica Herthel and Jazz Jennings

The story of a transgender child based on the real-life experience of Jazz Jennings, who has become a spokesperson for trans kids everywhere.

Good Pictures Bad Pictures: Porn-Proofing Today's Young Kids

Kristen A Jenson and Gail Poyner

An easy to read and understand book to help your kids learn about pornography including what it is and what to do when they see it. And they *will* see it!

For ages 10 and older

It's Perfectly Normal! Changing Bodies, Growing Up, Sex and Sexual Health

Robie Harris and Michael Emberley

The older kids' version of Robie and Michael's other books, this book is for kids 10 and older. It covers puberty, masturbation, sex, sexuality, same-sex relationships, birth control, STIs and HIV, pregnancy, birth, and healthy relationships. It contains everything they need to before middle school in a simple, easy-to-read package.

The "What's Happening to My Body?" Book for Girls – A Growing Up Guide for Preteen and Teens

Lynda Madaras with Area Madaras

This book includes many details about the changes of puberty, information about sex, sexual feelings, birth control, and STIs and HIV.

What's Going on Down There? Answers to Questions Boys Find Hard to Ask

Karen Gravelle with Nick and Chava Castro

This thoughtful book for boys explains in detail the changes of puberty, sex and sexual feelings, masturbation, birth control, and STIs and HIV. It includes interviews with men, who reflect on their own experiences during puberty and adolescence.

For ages 14 and older

Dating Smarts: What Every Teen Needs to Know to Date, Relate or Wait!

Amy Lang, MA

Want me to talk to your kids? Here you go. This is what they need to be clear about their sexual values and make smart choices about dating and sex. And waiting.

Body Drama – Real Girls, Real Bodies, Real Issues, Real Answers

Nancy Redd

I love this book. Written by a former Miss Virginia and Harvard graduate, it's a great book for girls. It presents information in a lively, readable fashion and includes many photographs so girls can see what's normal. Nancy Redd rocks!

Spare me 'the talk!': A Guy's Guide to Sex, Relationships, and Growing Up

Jo Langford, MA

Written by my friend and colleague, this is the only modern "guys only" book currently on the market. The first book of its kind by a guy, for guys ages 12-24, and for parents of boys as young as 8.

Spare Me 'The Talk'!: A <u>Girl's</u> Guide to Sex, Relationships, and Growing Up

Jo Langford, MA

Jo does it again! The first book about sexuality written by a guy, for girls. This book is the first of its kind for girls and young women ages 12-24, and for parents of girls as young as 8.

What Hollywood Won't Tell You About Sex, Love and Dating

Greg Johnson and Susie Shellenberger

A great book for teens from a Christian perspective. Greg and Susie offer sound advice for waiting to have sex, saying no, dating, and being clear about your values.

Recommended reading for adults

So Sexy, So Soon – The New Sexualized Childhood and What Parents Can Do to Protect Their Kids

Diane E. Levin, PH. D and Jean Kilbourne, Ed.D.

This book is a must read for every parent. Go get it from the library. Now.

The Talk: What Your Kids Need to Hear from You About Sex

Sharon Maxwell, Ph.D.

Short and to the point, Dr. Maxwell's book covers how our hypersexualized world is impacting children's sexuality, how to manage the internet and TV, the importance of sexual desire and the power of sex.

Everything You Never Wanted Your Kids to Know about Sex (But Were Afraid They'd Ask): The Secrets to Surviving Your Child's Sexual Development from Birth to the Teens

Justin Richardson and Mark Schuster

My all-time favorite book for parents; these guys know their stuff. It's very readable, funny and full of good ideas and stories about talking to kids about sex. This book will help make the conversations easier.

Sex and Sensibility: The Thinking Parent's Guide to Talking Sense about Sex

Deborah Roffman

A bit denser and tougher to read than my all-time favorite, Roffman's book offers sound ideas for parents to help you prepare for and tackle this important part of parenting.

Protecting the Gift, Keeping Children and Teenagers Safe (and Parents Sane)

Gavin De Becker

This is a wonderful book that explains the importance of helping our kids be savvy when they are out in the world. It's sometimes disturbing, but De Becker knows his stuff and really helps parents learn how to keep kids safe.

Smut: A Sex Industry Insider (and Concerned Father) Says Enough is Enough

Gil Reavill

This dad tells the tale of pornography and its impact on our kids, families, and culture. He knows what he's talking about – he worked in the industry as a writer.

Pornified: How Pornography is Damaging Our Lives, Our Relationships, and Our Families

Pamela Paul

The title says it all.

The Primal Teen: What the New Discoveries about the Teenage Brain Tell Us about Our Kids

Barbara Strauch

This book explains what is going on inside that crazy teen brain. Strauch explains neurology and how the brain works in a concise, fairly easy to read book.

Positive Discipline A-Z: 1001 Solutions to Everyday Parenting Problems

Jane Nelsen, Lynn Lott, and Stephen Glenn

The definitive guide to parenting from the heart, this book will help your kids behave better and you become a better parent.

ONLINE RESOURCES

Child Sexual Abuse Prevention + Information

StopItNow.org – Information on sexual abuse, child sexual development, red flags in adults, telephone hotline for instant support.

ChildMolestationPrevention.org – The Child Molestation Research and Prevention Institute

SavvyParentsSafeKids.com – Non-scary and pragmatic tips for keeping kids safe when they are out and about in the big wide world.

How to talk to kids about sex and general sexuality information

AdvocatesForYouth.org – Research on teen pregnancy, support for parents and includes information for all teens and young adults.

SIECUS.org – The Sexuality Information and Education Council of the United States. Research and information on just about everything related to sexuality.

TheNationalCampaign.org – National Campaign to Prevent Teen and Unwanted Pregnancy. All kinds of information to help everyone make better choices when it comes to pregnancy prevention.

CDC.gov – Centers for Disease Control. Up to the minute information on sexually transmitted infections.

Lesbian, Gay, Bi, Transgender, Queer/Questioning (LGBTQ) resources

ItGetsBetter.org – Testimonials from LGBTQ adults from all walks of life to support and encourage gay kids.

PFLAG.org – Parents And Friends Of Lesbians And Gays. Support for friends and families of LGBTQ kids.

GenderDiversity.com – For families with gender fluid and transgender kiddos.

Internet safety

Zoo.com – Kid-safe browser.

NetSmartz.org –National Center for Missing and Exploited Children. Find out current stats and how to keep kids safe from abduction.

IKeepSafe.org – Internet Keep Safe Coalition. Games and activities for younger kids and parents.

Qustodio.com – Internet monitoring software that can be installed on every device. I use it and it's great.

Pornography

FightTheNewDrug.com – More info on the impact of pornography. However, they are porn abstinence-only for everyone, no matter what, and I don't fully agree with their philosophy.

More Birds + Bees + Kids® resources

BirdsandBeesandKids.com – Birds + Bees + Kids® - my website for ordering resources, scheduling talks, professional trainings, workshops, and one-on-one consultations.

BirdsAndBeesCourse.com – my deeper-dive, online class for parents. Use code BEES for 20% off.

References

National Campaign to Prevent Teen And Unplanned Pregnancy. Fast Facts: Teen Pregnancy In The United States, Washington, DC: Accessed November 7, 2014.

Advocates for Youth, Abstinence-Only-Until-Marriage Programs: Ineffective, Unethical, and Poor Public Health, http://www.advocatesforyouth.org/publications/policybrief/pbabonly.htm. Accessed August, 22, 2008.

Laura Duberstein Lindberg, Ph.D. and others, Non-coital Sexual Activities Among Adolescents, Journal of Adolescent Health, May 2008.

Advocates for Youth, Young People and HIV, http://www.advocatesforyouth.org/publications/factsheet/fshivaid.html. Accessed October 17, 2008.

Center for Disease Control, HIV/AIDS Among Youth, http://www.cdc.gov/hiv/risk/age/youth/index.html?s_cid=tw_std0141316. Accessed November 6, 2014.

Kaiser Family Foundation, Generation M2: Media In The Lives of 8-To 18-Year Olds, http://kff.org/other/report/generation-m2-media-in-the-lives-of-8-to-18-year-olds/ Accessed November 6, 2014.

Guttmacher Institute, Facts Sheet: Induced Abortion in the United States, http://www.guttmacher.org/pubs/fb_induced_abortion.html, Accessed November 8, 2014.

Hanna Rosin, Why Kids Sext, http://www.theatlantic.com/magazine/archive/2014/11/why-kids-sext/380798/ The Atlantic. Accessed November 9, 2014.

Stop It Now, Age Appropriate Sexual Behavior In Children, http://www.stopitnow.org/age_appropriate_sexual_behavior Accessed November 9, 2014.

Sam Killerman, The Genderbread Person 2.0, http://itspronouncedmetrosexual.com/2012/03/the-genderbread-person-v2-0/ Accessed November 5, 2014.

Dear Reader:

Thank you so much for reading my book! I sincerely hope that it helps you have amazing, fun and effective conversations with your children about sexuality.

I am so grateful to you because you (yes YOU!) are helping me achieve my dream-mission of helping *every* kid grow up to be a whole and healthy adult. Your kid, my kid, kids in the US, France, Zimbabwe, on Mars... you name it. All the kids!

I believe that having a deep, healthy and values-based understanding of sexuality is the key to making this happen.

And, this is a huge undertaking, so I need a favor – but only if it feels right and good to you. No pressure. Seriously.

Can you please share my websites, my Facebook page, my words of wisdom, my books with the parents in your immediate circle? Just your besties, that's it!

> **BirdsAndBeesAndKids.com** – my general site for all things sex ed!

> **BirdsAndBeesCourse.com** – my deeper-dive, online class for parents. Use code *BEES* for 20% off.

> **Facebook.com/BirdsBeesKids** – my daily-ish sexuality updates, including Facebook Live sessions, tips, tricks and funny business related to sexuality education.

Thank you for helping me achieve my dream and helping every kid grow up healthy, happy and safe!

Amy Lang, MA

49350259R00068

Made in the USA
Middletown, DE
13 October 2017